WHAT DOES A GOVERNOR DO?

We the People: State and Local Government at Work

Published in the United States of America by:

Cherry Lake Press
2395 South Huron Parkway, Suite 200, Ann Arbor, Michigan 48104
www.cherrylakepress.com

Reading Adviser: Beth Walker Gambro, MS, Ed., Reading Consultant, Yorkville, IL
Content Adviser: Mark Richards, Ph.D., Professor, Dept. of Political Science, Grand Valley State University, Allendale, MI

Photo Credits: © Monkey Business Images/Shutterstock, cover, title page; © JARIRIYAWAT/Shutterstock, 5; © lev radin/Shutterstock, 6; © Sheila Fitzgerald/Shutterstock, 7; © Andrew Angelov/Shutterstock, 9; © lev radin/Shutterstock, 9; © imging/Shutterstock, 10–11; © ARMMY PICCA/Shutterstock, 12; © Gorodenkoff/Shutterstock, 13; © lev radin/Shutterstock, 14; © Dragana Gordic/Shutterstock, 15; © Ryan Rodrick Beiler/Shutterstock, 16; © James Housand/Shutterstock, 19; © Pressmaster/Shutterstock, 20; © Ground Picture/Shutterstock, 21

Cherry Lake Press is an imprint of Cherry Lake Publishing Group.

Library of Congress Cataloging-in-Publication Data has been filed and is available at catalog.loc.gov.

Cherry Lake Press would like to acknowledge the work of the Partnership for 21st Century Learning, a Network of Battelle for Kids. Please visit Battelle for Kids online for more information.

Printed in the United States of America

CONTENTS

Chapter 1: What Is a Governor? 4

Chapter 2: The Governor's Duties 10

Chapter 3: The Governor in National Politics 17

Activity 20
Glossary 22
Find Out More 23
Index 24
About the Author 24

WHAT IS A GOVERNOR?

One of the most powerful **elected officials** in your state is the governor. The governor is like the president of a state. Like the U.S. president, a governor's main job is to make sure that people follow the law. He or she has special powers in government. For example, when the lawmakers want to pass a law, the governor can decide against it. This decision is called a **veto**.

The governor needs to approve laws passed by the legislature.

Governors are elected by voters in the state. Citizens choose which governor they want.

States have rules about who can be a governor. In many states, a **candidate** for governor has to live in that state for at least a year. In many states, a candidate has to be at least 30 years old. In other states, they have to be at least 18.

Kathy Hochul (left) became governor of New York in 2021. Gavin Newsom (right) is California's 40th governor.

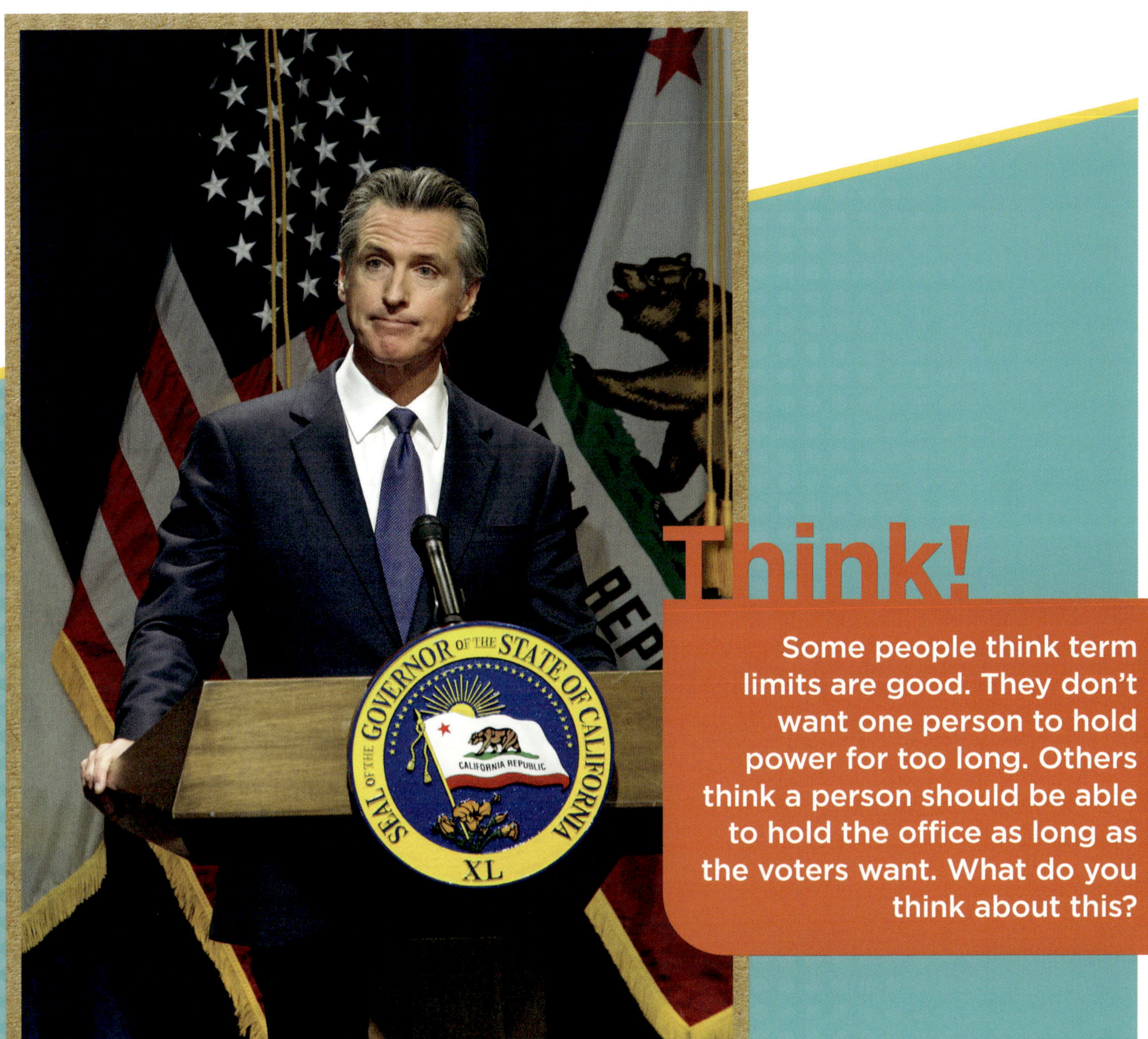

Think!

Some people think term limits are good. They don't want one person to hold power for too long. Others think a person should be able to hold the office as long as the voters want. What do you think about this?

Governors usually serve 4-year **terms**. This means they hold the job for 4 years. They will have to be reelected if they want to be governor again. Some states have **term limits**. This means you cannot be governor forever.

Ask Questions!

Governors make hard choices during a state of emergency. They have to act fast. They might need to provide money, food, or shelter for many people. They have to decide who to help first. Write down two questions for your governor about making decisions during an emergency.

Governors make tough decisions to guide their states through hard times. After storms, fires, or disease outbreaks, the governor has the power to declare a **state of emergency**. This official situation gives the governor power to spend money quickly.

Kathy Hochul kept New Yorkers updated during the COVID-19 pandemic. She had to make important decisions.

THE GOVERNOR'S DUTIES

What else does a governor do?

Governors can suggest new laws. As a state's leader, they have ideas about how to make life better in the state. They work with the state **legislature** to pass laws.

A governor is also commander of the state's National Guard. They can call on members of the state **militia** to protect people.

State judges make sure laws follow the state's constitution.

In some states, the governor can **appoint** judges. Judges make many important decisions. Some decisions affect only a few people. Some decisions affect many people. Judges must be fair to everyone.

Create!

Governors have their own ideas. They also need to listen to ideas from the people. Think about an issue you care about. Write a short letter to your governor. Explain why they should care about this topic too.

Governors sign state bills into law.

Make a Guess!

The governor has many jobs. For example, they lead the state's programs for drivers, trains, and farmers. They choose people to help them lead these programs. What do you think would happen if the governor didn't ask for help?

The governor can also grant **pardons**. If someone in jail is pardoned, that person can be freed from jail.

Governors lead different state programs, like the Department of Health. They work to make sure people have the health care they need.

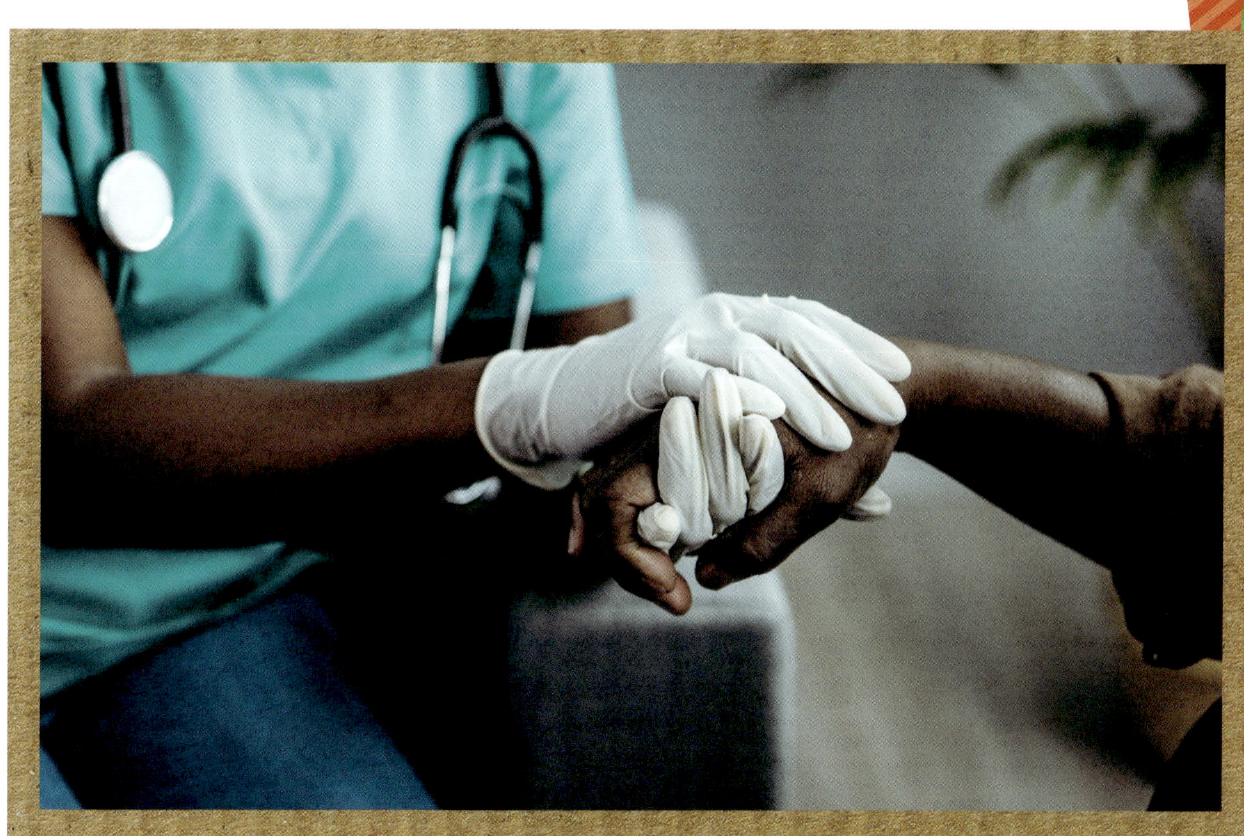

Health care is a national issue that states have an important role in.

THE GOVERNOR IN NATIONAL POLITICS

Governors take care of their own states. They also care what happens in the whole country. People may talk to their governors about national issues like immigration or health care.

Governors listen to the people in their state. Then they may talk to the president or the U.S. Congress. Governors may ask them to create **policies** or laws about these issues.

Look!

Many U.S. presidents have also been governors. Of the 46 presidents, 17 of them were once governors. Why do you think this is? What are some things a governor might learn that would help them be a good president?

Former president Ronald Reagan served as governor of California from 1967–1975.

ACTIVITY

INVESTIGATE! Who is your governor? Look at their official website and make a list of their duties. Pick one that you want to learn more about. Ask a family member, teacher, or librarian to help you understand the topic. Write down the most surprising thing you learned.

GLOSSARY

appoint (uh-POYNT) to select to fill an office or job

candidate (KAN-duh-dayt) a person running for an elected government position

elected officials (ih-LEK-tuhd uh-FIH-shuhlz) government workers chosen by vote of the people

legislature (LEH-juh-slay-cher) part of the state government that creates and passes laws

militia (muh-LIH-shuh) armed forces at the state level, such as the National Guard

pardons (PAHR-duhnz) official releases from legal punishment for crimes

policies (PAH-luh-seez) official rules

state of emergency (STAYT UV ee-MUR-juhn-see) a time when the government is given more power to help and protect people, such as during a natural disaster

terms (TURMZ) set lengths of time; for example, the length of time an elected official holds a position

term limits (TURM LIH-muhts) limits on the number of times an elected official can hold a position

veto (VEE-toh) to stop a bill from becoming a law

FIND OUT MORE

Books

Bedesky, Baron. *What is a Government?* New York, NY: Crabtree Publishing Co., 2008.

Christelow, Eileen. *Vote!* New York, NY: Clarion Books, 2018.

Let's Go Local!: Role of Branches in Local Government in the US. Baby Professor, 2022.

Websites

Search these online sources with an adult.

Local Government for Kids | Miacademy Learning Channel | YouTube
Learn how local government works.

iCivics
Find out how you can be an informed and involved citizen.

INDEX

activities, 20
agencies, 14, 15

California governors, 7, 11, 19
candidates for governor, 6

decision making, 4, 8, 9, 12

elections, 6, 8
emergencies, 8, 9

health care, 15, 16
Hochul, Kathy, 6, 9, 14

judges, 12–13

laws
  elections, 6
  passing, 4, 5, 10, 18
  veto power, 4

national government, 4, 17–18
National Guard, 10
natural disaster relief, 8, 9
Newsom, Gavin, 7
New York governors, 6, 9, 14

pardon power, 15
presidents, 4, 18–19

Reagan, Ronald, 19
roles and responsibilities, 4, 8, 9, 10–15, 17–18

Schwarzenegger, Arnold, 11
state government
  elections, 6, 8
  governors, 4–20
  judicial branch, 12–13
  legislators and laws, 4, 5, 10
  programs, 14, 15

terms and term limits, 7, 8

veto power, 4

ABOUT THE AUTHOR

Kevin Winn is a children's book writer and researcher. He focuses on issues of racial justice and educational equity in his work. In 2020, Kevin earned his doctorate in Educational Policy and Evaluation from Arizona State University.